Not by Bread Alone

Daily Reflections

Jay Cormier

LITURGICAL PRESS

Collegeville, Minnesota

www.litpress.org

Nihil Obstat: Rev. Robert C. Harren, J.C.L., *Censor deputatus.*

Imprimatur: ✠ Most Rev. John F. Kinney, J.C.D., D.D., Bishop of St. Cloud, Minnesota, July 24, 2009.

Cover design by Ann Blattner.

ISSN: 1552-8782
ISBN: 978-0-8146-3266-6

For Elaine and Tom Coronis

Introduction

[N]ot by bread alone does man live,
but by every word that comes forth from the mouth of the LORD.

The prophet's words from Deuteronomy (Deut 8:3) serve as a mantra for us Lenten pilgrims.

The challenge of this mantra is to strain to hear the voice of God speaking to us in the noisy din of our everyday lives. What we sometimes fail to realize is that God speaks to us in many languages, in many media. God speaks in every birth and in every death. God speaks in every experience of love and in every encounter with disaster. God speaks in the simplest act of kindness and in the most complex miracle of nature. God speaks in the brightest daylight and in the darkest night. God speaks in our loves, in our discoveries, in our disappointments, in our hurts, in our despair.

This collection of reflections for Lent 2010 attempts to capture the "words" spoken by God in the many facets of the human experience. The stories and images on the pages that follow are one traveler's attempt to uncover God's compassion in the human condition in all its wonder, messiness, and confusion. The poet Elizabeth Barrett Browning captured this idea beautifully: "Earth's crammed with heaven, / And every common bush is afire with God."

Let the Spirit of God open your hearts to hear every word God speaks in your midst in the days ahead. May the pieces of heaven in our here and now become bread for your journey with Christ to Easter hope.

February 17: Ash Wednesday

Spring Cleaning, Lenten Planting

Readings: Joel 2:12-18; 2 Cor 5:20–6:2; Matt 6:1-6, 16-18

Scripture:
Even now, says the LORD,
    return to me with your whole heart,
    with fasting, and weeping, and mourning;
Rend your hearts, not your garments,
    and return to the LORD, your God. (Joel 2:12-13)

Reflection: Today we begin our annual Lenten pilgrimage with ashes. As our brothers and sisters in the faith have done since antiquity, we place ashes on our heads as signs acknowledging our sinfulness and our mortality.

There are two particular properties of ashes that add to our understanding of the Easter mystery we anticipate during this holy season.

At one time, ashes were used to make soap. Ashes contain alkali, a soluble chemical that is a powerful cleaning agent. Let this Lent, then, be a time of cleaning and purification— a washing away of the grime of selfishness, hatred, and mistrust in our lives, a spring cleaning of all those things and attitudes that draw our attention away from God and the things of God.

In some places at this time of year, farmers burn the stubble of last year's crops that remain in the field. The remaining ashes are then plowed into the earth. The chemicals in the ashes serve as a powerful fertilizer for the new crops soon to be planted. Let this Lent, then, be a planting season for our souls and spirits—a time for the word of God to take root in our lives, a growing season for our hearts and spirits to be transformed from barrenness to harvest, from despair to hope, from death to life.

Meditation: Is there some situation in your life that you would like to wash away or make clean with a new beginning this Lent? What would you like to grow in its place?

Prayer: Gracious God, may we begin our forty days' Lenten springtime by embracing the meaning of these ashes. As we were once washed in the waters of baptism, may the word of your Son clean us again of our sins and purify us in hope and joy. During these early spring days, may your word take root in us, that we may know the harvest of your mercy and compassion in every season of every year.

February 18: Thursday after Ash Wednesday

Carnival: Putting Death to Death

Readings: Deut 30:15-20; Luke 9:22-25

Scripture:
"If anyone wishes to come after me, he must deny himself
and take up his cross daily and follow me.
For whoever wishes to save his life will lose it,
but whoever loses his life for my sake will save it."

(Luke 9:23-24)

Reflection: In New Orleans, Quebec City, and many other cities around the world, this has been carnival week. If you've ever experienced carnival, you know what a wild time it can be.

Carnival celebrations go back centuries before Christ. Like many pagan customs and celebrations, the early church "baptized" them, adapting them as celebrations of their young faith. For the first generations of Christians, the early spring festivals became a prelude to the solemn observance of Lent. The wild debauchery of Mardi Gras contrasted to the stark fast of Ash Wednesday. In fact, one of the merriest and funniest parts of carnival makes a very important point about the holiest and most sobering dimensions of Lent.

The end of carnival is marked by putting death to death. With infinite imagination and creativity, carnival celebrants depict death as an ugly devil, a grumpy Old Man Winter, or the king of fools. On the last night of carnival—Mardi Gras—

this figure of death is tossed into a lake or chased from the town or reduced to ashes during a midnight bonfire.

When death dies, carnival comes to an immediate end. Masks are removed, greasepaint is wiped off, the revelries cease. The past is left behind in ashes. Everything that is false and deceptive has been destroyed or exiled. The symbols of destruction are themselves destroyed.

The giving up of one's favorite confection or pastime notwithstanding, the most difficult dimension of Lent is to lay aside the masks we wear to hide not only from others but from ourselves as well. Lent demands a painful honesty from each one of us: yes, we are sinners, we are less than the people we want to be; but yes, we hunger to change, we want to transform our lives into becoming what God has called us to be. As we begin our pilgrimage toward Easter, may we rediscover the world, not through the eyes of our carnival masks, but through the eyes of Easter faith.

Meditation: Is there a mask you would like to remove or a tension you would like to put to death this Lenten season?

Prayer: Father of new beginnings, let this Lenten season be a new beginning for us. Help us to put to death the sins that diminish us, to wipe away the arrogance and selfishness that alienate us from you and from others, to remove our masks of deception and dishonesty that prevent us from becoming the people you have called us to be. With new hearts and spirits, may we rise at the end our Lenten journey to the new life of your Risen Christ.

The Parable of the King

Readings: Isa 58:1-9a; Matt 9:14-15

Scripture:
"Can the wedding guests mourn
as long as the bridegroom is with them?" (Matt 9:15)

Reflection: A certain king was very rich and powerful. But he was most unhappy, for he desired a wife. Without a queen, his vast palace was empty.

One day, while riding through the streets of a small village, he saw a beautiful peasant girl. Her beauty immediately won the heart of the king.

The king wondered how he might win her love. First, he thought of issuing a royal decree commanding her to be his bride, but he soon realized that if she were forced to obey a royal decree as a loyal subject, the king could never be certain that she loved him.

Next he considered calling on the woman in person, overwhelming her with diamonds and silver and all kinds of royal finery, but he knew he would always wonder whether she had married him only for the riches and power he could give her.

Then he thought about dressing as a peasant and going to meet her in disguise, but such a plan was too dishonest for the king.

The king finally decided to shed his royal robes, put aside his wealth and power, and actually become one of the peasants. He lived and worked and suffered alongside them. And, in the end, he won the young woman as his queen.

The Danish philosopher Soren Kierkegaard used this parable to articulate the mystery of Christ, the incarnate Word-made-flesh, who loved us enough to "shed" his own divinity and live and suffer alongside us, all in order to bring us to himself. The focus of this holy season is God's "shedding" his divinity and becoming one of us in all our poverty, in all our stumbling, in all our despair. In the mystery of the incarnation, the incomparable love of God becomes enfleshed in the person of the gospel Jesus. As St. Irenaeus wrote, "Because of his great love for us, Jesus, the Word of God, became what we are in order to make us what he is himself."

Meditation: Where can you see and hear the bridegroom Christ present in your life?

Prayer: O Christ the Bridegroom, give us the vision of faith and charity of heart to recognize your presence among us in one another. May we honor you in our compassion and love for each other: in our washing the feet of one another, in helping each other bear our crosses of sorrow and pain, in giving to one another without counting the cost or without expecting anything in return. May your presence among us be the light that guides us at last to your wedding banquet in the kingdom of your Father.

February 20: Saturday after Ash Wednesday

Planting Faith

Readings: Isa 58:9b-14; Luke 5:27-32

Scripture:
"I have not come to call the righteous to repentance but sinners." (Luke 5:32)

Reflection: When you think about it, planting a seed is an incredible act of faith.

Imagine: a tiny seed or a handful of tiny seeds becoming, within a matter of weeks, a harvest of fruits and vegetables, a garden of beautiful flowers, a rich green lawn.

With great hope and expectation, you purchase your envelope of seeds and read all that needs to be done. As you place the seed in a small hole or scatter the seed in the wet earth, you wonder, especially if you are a novice gardener, if anything will happen. You water and fertilize, you hoe and weed, for what seems like an eternity. You resign yourself to the possibility that your new lawn will never look like the fairway at Augusta, that your garden will never appear on the cover of *Better Homes and Gardens*.

But then, just when you least expect it or you've given up hope, the first green blades appear, then the stalks, then the branches, then the first fruit.

You are now a believer in the miracle—the miracle of a single seed.

This Lenten springtime calls us to such faith: that love can spring forth from barrenness, that there is reason to hope in the midst of despair, that light can and will dawn to shatter our overwhelming sense of loneliness and sadness. The Risen One promises us that the seeds of joy, trust, and community that we plant even in the hardest soil and nurture in the coldest winters will take root and blossom and yield a miraculous harvest.

Meditation: What hard soil in your life needs to be broken in order for a new sense of purpose and joy to spring up?

Prayer: Gracious God, giver of all life, plant the seed of your word within our broken hearts. During this Lenten season, may your word take root in us, that we may know the harvest of your joy and mercy in every season of every year.

February 21: First Sunday of Lent

Dakota

Readings: Deut 26:4-10; Rom 10:8-13; Luke 4:1-13

Scripture:
Filled with the Holy Spirit, Jesus returned from the Jordan
and was led by the Spirit into the desert for forty days,
to be tempted by the devil. (Luke 4:1-2a)

Reflection: Thirty years ago Kathleen Norris and her husband David returned to her family's home in Lemmon, South
Dakota, to live in the house her grandparents built in 1923.
The experience led her to a new understanding and appreciation of the many ways in which God reveals himself in the
ordinary and simple. Her return to her roots led the little-
practicing Presbyterian to discover Benedictine spirituality
at a nearby Catholic monastery. She writes about the "holy
ground" of the Great Plains and its influence on the human
spirit in her best-selling book *Dakota: A Spiritual Geography*:

> The Great Plains themselves have become my monastery,
> my place set apart, where I thrive and grow. It surprises me
> also to find that I no longer need to visit the city—any city—to
> obtain what I am missing, because I don't feel deprived. . . .
> It was the Plains that first drew me to the monastery, which
> I suppose is ironic, for who would go seeking a desert within
> a desert? Both Plains and monastery are places where distrac-
> tions are at a minimum and you must rely on your own

resources, only to find yourself utterly dependent on forces beyond your control; where time seems to stand still, as it does in the liturgy; where your life is defined by waiting. No one waits better than monks, or farmers.

We begin this season of Lent in a place set apart, similar to Norris's beloved Dakota. After being baptized by John in the River Jordan, Jesus went off to the quiet and peace of the wilderness where he spent forty days discerning exactly what it means to be the Christ and what God was calling him to do as the Messiah. The same Spirit that led Jesus into the wilderness leads us into this forty-day wilderness experience of Lent to ask ourselves the same kind of questions about our identity as the people of God, to begin to understand who we are and what we are becoming. Lent is a time for us to discern what God calls us to be so that we may recenter our lives with renewed hope in the fulfillment of the promise of the resurrection in our own lives.

Meditation: Is there a "desert place" you can go to this Lent, a quiet place where you can spend time reconnecting with God?

Prayer: Lead us, O Lord, into the desert of our hearts this Lent. Open our hearts to the promptings of your Spirit that these desert days may be a time of discernment and conversion. May Jesus be our companion as we journey this Lent from the desert of commitment to the fulfillment of Easter in your holy city of peace.

Knowing . . .

Readings: 1 Pet 5:1-4; Matt 16:13-19

Scripture:
[Jesus] said to [his disciples], "But who do you say that
    I am?"
Simon Peter said in reply,
    "You are the Christ, the Son of the living God."
(Matt 16:15-16)

Reflection: In his book *Overcoming Life's Disappointments*,
Rabbi Harold S. Kushner writes about a man whose wife
suffered from Alzheimer's disease. Every day she slipped
further and further away in the fog of dementia—but every
day he would come to spend time with her.

The couple's heartbroken friends would ask him, "Why do
you keep going when she doesn't even know who you are?"

And he would always reply, "Because I know who I am."

This husband's faithfulness is the perfect and complete
answer to the question Jesus poses to Peter and the others
in today's gospel. In realizing exactly who Jesus is and the
meaning of the Gospel he embodies, we start to understand
who we are and what our lives are about. Today's gospel
asks us exactly what we mean when we say that "I believe
in Jesus Christ, [God's] only Son, our Lord," what we mean
when we claim that we have been baptized into his death

and resurrection. Our love and compassion for family and friends, our dedication to what is right and just, our taking the first step toward reconciliation and forgiveness, our simplest acts of kindness and generosity are our confession of faith in the gospel Jesus as the Messiah and Redeemer.

On this Lenten Monday, we remember Peter's confession of faith. The fisherman is the first of Jesus' followers to acknowledge him as the Messiah. And it is on that faith that Jesus establishes his church of peace, reconciliation, and justice. To share Peter's faith in the gospel Jesus is to articulate clearly and without equivocation the answer to the question Jesus asks of all of us: "Who do you say I am?"

Meditation: What most recent action of yours do you see as your own response to the question Jesus poses to Peter and the others today?

Prayer: Risen Christ, give us the simple but profound faith of Peter. May we possess Peter's resolve to be worthy of your call to be your disciples; may we share his determination to build your church here in our time and place; may we embrace his perseverance to proclaim your presence in every moment you give us, in every decision that confronts us, in every relationship with which we are blessed.

The Responsible Parties

Readings: Isa 55:10-11; Matt 6:7-15

Scripture:
"This is how you are to pray:
'Our Father who art in heaven . . .
thy will be done,
    on earth as it is in heaven.'" (Matt 6:9, 10)

Reflection: After a great deal of difficulty and frustration, a young couple had finally conceived their first child—in fact, the young woman was pregnant with triplets. Her doctors insisted that she stay in bed for the duration of her pregnancy.

After their friends learned the exciting news, flowers and notes and cards filled their small house. After church, the pastor said to the husband, "We'll be praying for you two in these next few months."

The husband's response caught the pastor a little off guard. "Good," the father-to-be said. "And we're going to hold all of those who have said they will pray for us responsible."

Although the husband's response was meant to be in jest, it reflects an important understanding about prayer. Prayer is not about wrestling favors and gifts from an unwilling God; prayer is about trying to understand and accept God's will for us. In today's gospel, Jesus gives us much more than a formula of words—Jesus gives us the proper attitude for prayer: that true prayer is to seek God's will in all things; to give thanks for what God has given us by sharing those gifts with one another; to treasure love and forgiveness, mercy and reconciliation above all else.

The great English saint Thomas More captured the essence of prayer when he wrote, "Give us the grace, O Lord, to work for what we pray for."

Meditation: What prayer are you willing to work for?

Prayer: Father in heaven, do not let us confine our prayer to words and rituals alone. Open our hearts and inspire our spirits to work and sacrifice for the hopes and dreams we ask of you. May every moment you give us be part of a continuous lifelong prayer of praise to you, you who are the Giver and Sustainer of all life.

Sign Values

Readings: Jonah 3:1-10; Luke 11:29-32

Scripture:
"Just as Jonah became a sign to the Ninevites,
   so will the Son of Man be to this generation." (Luke 11:30)

Reflection: The child is fascinated by numbers. The little number blocks are a powerful new tool. Soon the boy or girl can count the coins in the child's piggy bank, measure paper and wood to create all kinds of things, play—and win—all kinds of new games with his knowledge of numbers. In learning the signs of numbers, the child discovers what it means to keep score, to measure outcomes, and to possess things—and even more things.

When the child becomes a student, he or she learns the deeper meaning of those number signs. After much study, the student can devise plans for buildings and bridges, roads and waterways; compute the necessary logarithms to send a spaceship to a distant planet; calculate the perfect formula to create the strongest plastic, the most effective detergent, the best-tasting ketchup. In mastering the number signs, the student acquires power.

And then the student becomes a scientist, learning to harness the power of those number signs. Now comes the most critical decision of all: *What will I do with the power of these signs?* Make a great deal of money? Amass an overwhelming degree of control and wealth? Or use the power of these signs to create a safer, cleaner, and healthier world? To bring hope and healing, sustenance and empowerment to the poor, the sick, the unskilled? To create products that will benefit the common good first and make a profit for stockholders second?

The child and student first must learn to read and master the signs; the scientist must then make the adult decision as to how to use the power of those signs—for oneself, or for something much greater.

To learn is to read and harness the power of signs: the signs of language, mathematics, molecular structure, the cycle of nature. In baptism, we are given a new set of signs to watch for, a new language to listen and respond to, a new table of values to discern. God calls us to watch for the unmistakable signs of his love in our midst, to listen for words and opportunities for forgiveness and reconciliation, to mark the moral and ethical icons of justice and mercy in our day-to-day lives.

Meditation: What signs of God's compassion and justice do you recognize in your life?

Prayer: Open our eyes and humble our spirits, Lord God, to see the signs of your love, justice, and forgiveness in our midst. May we, in turn, become effective signs of your compassionate presence in this time and place of ours, signs of your call to reconciliation, signs of your spirit of justice and mercy in the Ninevehs of our homes and schools and workplaces.

Pray and Trample

Readings: Esth C:12, 14-16, 23-25; Matt 7:7-12

Scripture:
"For everyone who asks, receives; and the one who seeks,
    finds;
   and to the one who knocks, the door will be opened."

(Matt 7:8)

Reflection: A little girl was telling her father about how some of the boys in the neighborhood had set traps to catch birds. He asked her what she did about it.

"I prayed that the traps might not catch the birds," she said.

"Anything else?" her father asked.

"I prayed that God would keep the birds out of the traps," she replied.

"Anything else?"

"When the boys weren't looking I went and kicked all the traps to pieces."

This determined little girl understands the meaning and purpose of prayer. In many of our prayers, we ask God to come around to doing our will—but true prayer is to discover God's will for *us*. We often approach prayer as trying to wring gifts from an unwilling, reluctant God; in fact, we come before a God who knows our needs better than we do ourselves.

Authentic prayer seeks to make God's will *our* will—and being ready and willing to make the necessary transformations in our everyday life to make our prayers a reality. Prayer worthy of God seeks the grace to do the work God calls us to do (forgiveness, charity, justice) and to become the people God calls us to become (brothers and sisters under the one heavenly Father).

Meditation: Of all the things you seek in your life, which ones are worthy of prayer?

Prayer: Good and gracious God, you know our needs and pains and emptiness before we even know them ourselves. Guide our hearts, that we may walk in your light as we travel through this lifetime; take our hands in yours and set them to the work of making our prayers for love, reconciliation, and justice realities in our time and place.

Welcome to Heaven. Your Table Is Ready.

Readings: Ezek 18:21-28; Matt 5:20-26

Scripture:
"[U]nless your righteousness surpasses that
of the scribes and Pharisees,
you will not enter into the Kingdom of heaven." (Matt 5:20)

Reflection: There was a dedicated old priest who had always wondered what the real difference was between heaven and hell. One day, he had a dream in which God showed him.

First, God showed him hell. The old priest was flabbergasted to find no flames, no horned, pointy-tailed devils—only crowds of angry people pressing around long picnic tables. At each place was a large wooden bowl of food and ten-foot-long wooden spoons. Pushing and shoving to find places at the tables, the angry people managed to get their long spoons into the bowls—but they were unable to turn the spoons around and get them into their mouths. Their frustration and the accompanying bitterness and bickering were sheer hell!

Then the old priest was given a glimpse of heaven. He was amazed to discover the same massive picnic tables, the same huge wooden bowls of food, and the same ten-foot-long wooden spoons. But in heaven there was a spirit of peace, thoughtfulness, even joy. In heaven, the people were feeding one another.

To enter the kingdom of God, to realize the reign of God among us in the here and now, we must embrace a new attitude toward God and one another, an attitude based on compassion, generosity, forgiveness, and justice, an attitude centered not in self but in the common good. Such is the holiness that Christ calls us to adopt in our lives if we are to be true sons and daughters of the Father, true brothers and sisters to one another, true disciples of the Risen One.

Meditation: In what concrete if small way can you make the kingdom of heaven a reality in your own home or community?

Prayer: Father in heaven, make us worthy to one day reside in your dwelling place by embracing your spirit of love and compassion for one another on our journey to you. As you feed us, may we feed one another; as you forgive us, may we forgive one another; as you welcome us into your presence at the end of time, may we welcome one another to our tables in this time you have given us.

Let Even the Jerk Be Received as Christ

Readings: Deut 26:16-19; Matt 5:43-48

Scripture:
"But I say to you, love your enemies,
   and pray for those who persecute you,
   that you may be children of your heavenly Father,
   for he makes his sun rise on the bad and the good,
   and causes rain to fall on the just and the unjust."

(Matt 5:44-45)

Reflection: St. Bernard, one of the great abbots in Benedictine history, gave this rather startling advice to the monasteries he founded and led: "If ever there should be a monastery without a troublesome and bad-tempered member, it would be necessary to find one and pay him his weight in gold because of the great profit that results from this trial, when good use is made of it."

Wise Abbot Bernard understood the point of Jesus' words in today's gospel: that the cutting edge of the Gospel is forgiveness and tolerance, that what marks us as men and women of faith is our realizing that we are all sinners before God, that we are called not to be God's surrogate judges or "hammers" on earth but to be God's agents of forgiveness and justice and reconciliation.

God knows, it's not easy. But, in the spirit of St. Bernard, let us welcome into our midst the jerk, the whiner, and the weasel and, out of faithfulness to our call and gratitude for what we have received, let them know that they too—despite themselves—are loved by God. In our halting attempts to love the unlovable, in including in our work or play those whom we would rather have nothing to do with, we gain some small insight into the depth and breadth of God's love, a love that embraces every soul.

Even the likes of them.

And even the likes of us.

Meditation: Is there someone in your life whom you find especially difficult to love? How can you create a better relationship with that individual?

Prayer: Lord Jesus, open our hearts and spirits to see you in everyone. Help us to get beyond what annoys and angers us in others and accept gratefully the gifts they possess. Give us the patience and openness of heart to be forgiving of others as you are forgiving of us. May we praise you and proclaim your Gospel in our graciousness and kindness toward the ungracious and unkind among us.

The Music Within

Readings: Gen 15:5-12, 17-18; Phil 3:17–4:1 or 3:20–4:1;
Luke 9:28b-36

Scripture:
While [Jesus] was praying his face changed in appearance
   and his clothing became dazzling white.
And behold, two men were conversing with him, Moses
      and Elijah,
   who appeared in glory and spoke of his exodus
   that he was going to accomplish in Jerusalem.

(Luke 9:28-31)

Reflection: She had spent years studying her art: rehearsing, exercising, massaging her tired feet and aching leg muscles. She had danced many nights with many companies. But this night, she danced as she had never danced before. Even the usually caustic dance captain could not fail to notice. She danced as if she was possessed by the music. Her body and the music were inseparable. Her performance transcended the exacting choreography. She now danced from her heart.

It is said that the best dancers and musicians and artists are those who feel the beauty of their art within them: the dancer whose body becomes inseparable from the music, the musician whose playing captures not just the notes of the score but also the emotion and meaning within the work, the artist who creates with the eye of the heart.

Such artistic expressions are nothing less than experiences of transfiguration. In the gospel we have come to call Jesus' "transfiguration," Peter, James, and John see the divinity—the very life and love of God—that exists within the person of Jesus. They realize that within Jesus dwells a compassion and grace that will manifest itself in their rabbi's teachings, healings, and, ultimately, his resurrection.

That same divinity exists within each one of us as well: God is present within us, animating us to do what is right and just, guiding our steps as we try to walk justly and humbly in the ways of God, enlightening our vision with wisdom and self-lessness to bring the justice and mercy of God to our world. The challenge of discipleship is to allow the love of God within us to "transfigure" despair into hope, sadness into joy, anguish into healing, estrangement into community.

Meditation: What elements of "divinity"—the life of God—do you sense within yourself that you underestimate or overlook? And how can that sense of "divinity" you possess transfigure your life and world?

Prayer: May the light of your love illuminate our hearts, O God, that we may discover the sense of your divinity within ourselves. May that sacredness enable us to see beyond our own needs, wants, and interests so that we may set about to transfigure our lives and our world in your compassion, justice, and forgiveness.

March 1: Monday of the Second Week of Lent

The Gift

Readings: Dan 9:4b-10; Luke 6:36-38

Scripture:
"For the measure with which you measure
   will in return be measured out to you." (Luke 6:38)

Reflection: Once upon a time, a monk, in his travels, found a precious stone worth a great deal of money. The monk kept it wrapped in a cloth in his traveling bag.

Along the way, the monk met another traveler. As was the custom among the brothers, he offered to share his provisions with the stranger. As the monk opened his bag, the traveler saw the jewel and admired it. The monk readily gave the poor man the jewel. The traveler departed, overjoyed with the unexpected gift of the precious stone that would provide him and his family wealth and security for the rest of their lives.

But a few days later, the man sought out the monk at his abbey and returned the stone, begging the good brother: "I have come to ask you for something much more precious than this stone. Give me whatever enabled you to give it to me."

To be able to give not from our treasure but from our need, to see others as if they were Christ, to take without hesitation the first step in being reconciled with someone from whom we are estranged, to love and trust and console and raise up another regardless of the cost to us—this is the "ruler" against which Christ calls us to live our lives, the "yardstick" of compassion by which we will one day be measured.

Meditation: What values, beliefs, and principles make up the "yardstick" by which you measure your decisions and approaches to problems in your life?

Prayer: Father of compassion, give us the gift of your Spirit of love, gratitude, and forgiveness. Do not let self-interest and vengeance be the yardstick we employ in our lives, but help us to measure by your rule of compassion and justice.

The Cherished Raspberry

Readings: Isa 1:10, 16-20; Matt 23:1-12

Scripture:
"The greatest among you must be your servant."

(Matt 23:11)

Reflection: In Boston's downtown Quincy Market there is a memorial to the victims of the Holocaust. The memorial is made up of six pillars of Plexiglas. On the pillars, against a background of the millions of prisoner numbers assigned by the Nazis to those who perished, are recounted stories of the cruelty and suffering endured in the camps.

But one of the pillars recalls a different story. It is about a little girl named Ilse, a childhood friend of Gerda Weissman Klein, who tells the story. Gerda remembers the morning when Ilse, who was about six years old at the time of her internment at Auschwitz, found a single raspberry somewhere in the camp. Ilse carried the raspberry all day long in a protected fold of her pocket. That evening, her eyes shining with happiness, Ilse presented the raspberry on a leaf to her friend Gerda.

"Imagine a world," writes Gerda, "in which your entire possession is one raspberry, and you give it to your friend."

In the midst of the horror of the Holocaust, little Ilse managed to discover the joy that only comes from bringing joy to another. That is the call of Jesus to us this Lent: to find the incomparable joy that comes only by seeking and bringing joy to others, to discover the treasure that is ours by what we give away, to possess the honor and dignity that is centered in humble compassion and generosity. In his life of humble service to others, Christ teaches us that greatness in the kingdom of God belongs to those who are the servants of others, that authentic authority is grounded in an attitude of selfless compassion for the smallest and weakest, that the Son will exalt before his Father in heaven those who humble themselves to serve the common good of family, friends, and community.

Jesus calls us this Lent to seek compassion despite our own anxiety, forgiveness beyond our own hurts, justice beyond our own predicament, generosity beyond our own needs.

Meditation: In your own home, workplace, and school, consider ways you can embrace the attitude of the gospel servant.

Prayer: Father, may we experience the joy of being your servant to others. May we find our life's meaning and purpose in imitating your humble servanthood by working to banish envy, disappointment, and avarice from our lives and by seeking to bring healing and hope into every life we touch.

March 3: Wednesday of the Second Week of Lent

Conventional Wisdom

Readings: Jer 18:18-20; Matt 20:17-28

Scripture:
"You know that the rulers of the Gentiles lord it over them,
and the great ones make their authority over them felt.
But it shall not be so among you." (Matt 20:25-26)

Reflection: We all know the conventional wisdom:

It's a dog-eat-dog world out there. You've got to do it to them before they do it to you.

But it shall not be so among you . . .

Always remember the golden rule: Those who have the gold make the rules.

But it shall not be so among you . . .

Remember: Never get mad. Get even.

But it shall not be so among you . . .

Take my advice, kid: Don't make waves. You've got to go along to get along. Keep your eyes open and your mouth shut.

But it shall not be so among you . . .

The users and the abusers, the punks and the perverts—they're scum, a blight on society. They deserve what happens to them. We work hard for what we've got—nobody's doing us any favors. Let them do the same. Hey, look: you've got to take care of your own.

But it shall not be so among you . . .

Jesus' admonition in today's gospel is almost a pleading: "If you really understand me and what I am about, if you really want to be my disciple, if you really seek to be worthy of my name, then you must see things with a set a values that run counter to conventional wisdom." The world may try to justify vengeance rather than forgiveness, to glorify self-preservation over servanthood, to insist on preserving the system and convention for the sake of compassion and justice, but if the love and mercy of the reign of God is to be realized, it must be different with us, who would be disciples of the Risen One.

Meditation: Is there some bit of "conventional wisdom" that you would like to challenge in your own life?

Prayer: Father, inspire us with your Son's spirit of humility to realize that in serving others we serve you, that in giving to others we give thanks to you. Help us to embrace Jesus' attitude of joyful servanthood so that we may re-create our lives and world in your life and love.

Consumed

Readings: Jer 17:5-10; Luke 16:19-31

Scripture:
"There was a rich man who dressed in purple garments and
    fine linen
  and dined sumptuously each day.
And lying at his door was a poor man named Lazarus,
  covered with sores,
    who would gladly have eaten his fill of the scraps
    that fell from the rich man's table." (Luke 16:19-21)

Reflection: A strange but true fact from the sea that you
might find difficult to "digest": There is a species of jellyfish
found in the Italian Mediterranean that feeds on tiny snails
of the nudibranch variety. The snail is protected by its shell—
the jellyfish cannot digest them. So, once the jellyfish eats
one of these snails, a bizarre reversal of roles takes place: the
diner becomes the *dinner*. Attaching itself to the wall of the
jellyfish's digestive tract, the snail begins to eat the jellyfish.
By the time the snail grows to maturity, it has completely
consumed the jellyfish. The poor jellyfish is eventually consumed by what it has consumed.

What we consume can consume us as well: we can be
swallowed up in our pursuit of wealth, prestige, and power,
isolating us from family and friends, making us immune to

human feeling and emotion, desensitizing us to any other's needs but our own. The rich man in the story of Lazarus loses his soul not because he is rich but because he is so consumed by his wealth that he is immune to the plight of the Lazaruses at his gate.

Jesus' story of the rich man and Lazarus is a warning this Lent to be careful of the "snail" we consume that can swallow us up, displacing the eternal things of God with the immediate but fleeting in our lives.

Meditation: Is there anything in your life that isolates you from the plight of others, that you may not even realize you place before the feelings and needs of those around you?

Prayer: O God, giver of all that is good, do not let us be consumed by the good things of this world, but give us your grace to use them to create your kingdom of compassion, justice, and peace. Help us to realize the joy and sense of purpose that comes from giving to others as you give to us. In welcoming the poor at our own gates to our tables, may we welcome you; in giving to them from the bounty you have given us, may we return to you. Through the Lazaruses we meet and welcome, may we discover your joy in giving to others as you have given to us.

The Vineyard

Readings: Gen 37:3-4, 12-13a, 17b-28a; Matt 21:33-43, 45-46

Scripture:
"But when the tenants saw the son, they said to one another,
  'This is the heir.
Come, let us kill him and acquire his inheritance.'
They seized him, threw him out of the vineyard, and
  killed him." (Matt 21:38-39)

Reflection: In these difficult economic times for all of us, a
moment of hope from a Minnesota supermarket:

While a woman waited to check out at the grocery store,
the person ahead of her turned and handed her an envelope.
On the front there was a note: "There is $50 in this envelope
for your groceries. Take it if you need it or pass it on." She
passed the envelope to the person behind her, who in turn
gave it away. As she watched the envelope progress through
the lines she was surprised that some people even added
money to it.

The Spirit of God moved through that line of shoppers in
the form of an envelope. Any time compassion and generosity, selflessness and humility compel people to do what is
right and just, the Spirit of God is moving among them.

Today's gospel shows a "vineyard" devoid of that Spirit.
For the tenants, all that matters is the profit to be realized.

They turn on the vineyard owner who has been nothing but kind to them; they murder the owner's son who comes to hold them accountable.

We have seen what happens when the interests of the few are placed before the common good of all, when basic ethics and morality are dismissed as naive and unrealistic in order to make the quick buck. God will hold us accountable so that his vineyard will be used responsibly and justly for the good of all.

God has given us a wonderful vineyard that we often take for granted, that we mar and destroy by our selfishness. Christ comes with a new vision for the vineyard, a vision of generous sharing rather than obsessive taking, of peace rather than hostility, of forgiveness rather than vengeance. May we welcome Christ into the vineyard of our homes, our workplaces, our schools, aware that he calls us to the demanding conversion of the Gospel, but determined to sow and reap the blessings of God's reign.

Meditation: Have you ever put aside an ethical or moral principle for the sake of profit, convenience, or popularity?

Prayer: O Lord of the vineyard, you gave us this earth as a place of peace to seek you and grow in your love. By your grace, wisdom, and light, may we transform the villages and vineyards you have given us into places where your justice abounds and your peace reigns.

The Morning after the Party

Readings: Mic 7:14-15, 18-20; Luke 15:1-3, 11-32

Scripture:
"The servant said to [the older brother],
   'Your brother has returned
   and your father has slaughtered the fattened calf
   because he has him back safe and sound.'
He became angry,
   and when he refused to enter the house,
   his father came out and pleaded with him."

(Luke 15:27-28)

Reflection: So what about *after* the party?

What happened the next morning when the prodigal and his father and his still-seething brother faced one another during their first breakfast together in a long time?

Despite the joyous welcome home the day before, it must have been awkward, embarrassing, and tense. But forgiveness had been sought and given. It was a new beginning for this broken family.

That's important to understand. Forgiveness is not an end in itself; "I'm sorry" is not a quick fix; offering and accepting an apology doesn't automatically make everything all right. Sadly, forgiveness doesn't "forget." Forgiveness is that difficult first step on the long journey to reconciliation; forgiveness is the first balm in what can be a long, painful process of healing.

Reconciliation cannot begin until the prodigal humbles himself to admit the hurt he has caused and takes responsibility for what he has done.

Reconciliation is only possible because the father's loving, generous spirit enables him to let go of his hurt to welcome the prodigal home.

Reconciliation can only take place when the older brother makes room in his own heart for his brother to come home.

Then begins the hard work of restoring trust, of rebuilding the broken relationship, of repairing the damage that has been done.

The day before, the angry brother said to his father, "So your son is home. And that's it?"

Not by a long shot.

Meditation: What do you find is the most difficult part of forgiving another person or asking another for forgiveness?

Prayer: Father, help us to take on the hard work of forgiveness. May we imitate your own unconditional and limitless love by seeking to restore trust and mend the hurts that we have caused others and that others have inflicted on us. Help us to let go of our needs to justify our self-centeredness and demands for restitution and vengeance so that we may begin the work of restoring your gift of peace and unity among us.

I Love You. You're Under Arrest.

Readings: Exod 3:1-8a, 13-15; 1 Cor 10:1-6, 10-12; Luke 13:1-9. The readings for Year A may be read in place of these.

Scripture:
"'For three years now I have come in search of fruit on
    this fig tree
but have found none . . .'
'Sir, leave it for this year also,
and I shall cultivate the ground around it and fertilize it;
it may bear fruit in the future.
If not you can cut it down.'" (Luke 13:7, 8-9)

Reflection: We all love our children and would do anything for them. But do you love your son or daughter enough to have him or her arrested?

Actor Martin Sheen does.

Sheen's son Charlie's hard-driving life was out of control. Interventions and rehab had not worked. In May 1998, Charlie was hospitalized from a drug overdose. That's when his dad took the radical and, in the end, successful step of turning him in.

Martin Sheen recalls:

> "The only way I got Charlie, frankly, was because he'd skipped out of the hospital. I had to pay the bill. In paying the bill, I got to see why he was there. . . . It was the only way I got him.

"The critical part of the equation is: Are you willing to risk your child's wrath? They are not going to like you. Don't even think about them loving you. They're going to call you the most vicious, obscene names. You have to be prepared for that . . . [but] when a life is at stake and it's your child, you become fearless in a lot of ways."

Charlie Sheen got help. In a later interview he thanked his father "for saving my life."

Martin Sheen challenged his son to see the "root" of the issue: that we must be willing to accept the consequences of the choices we make. We may get away with it for a while, but eventually we have to confront who we are and what we really believe. Unless that kind of conversion takes place, we become like the barren fig tree: rootless, lifeless, giving nothing to others. The good news of the gospel fig tree is that, in taking responsibility for our actions and seeking to heal the hurt we have inflicted, we can again realize a harvest from our life's struggling fig trees.

Meditation: What is the most difficult reality you struggle to accept in your own life—and how can you readjust your thinking to better deal with it?

Prayer: God of new beginnings, you are the ever-patient gardener who nurtures our cracking and dried branches in the water of your love and the food of your compassion. Bind up our broken spirits in your grace and hope; nourish us by your grace and sustain us in your love that we may realize the harvest of your justice and peace in our lives.

The "Commitment" Move

Readings: 2 Kgs 5:1-15b; Luke 4:24-30

Scripture:
"[N]o prophet is accepted in his own native place."

(Luke 4:24)

Reflection: In rock climbing, it's called the "commitment move." It's the moment when you step off the secure rock ledge or crag you are standing on in order to move a little higher. Even though you're secured by ropes, it's a scary step. You must place your trust in what you're tied to rather than what you're standing on; you must "commit" to the unknown and unfamiliar if you are to continue your ascent.

Today's gospel offers the same kind of challenge: The God that we are connected to—by the Spirit of God, by sacrament, by prayer—is so much greater than the earth and the things of earth we stand on. The authentic prophet, the faithful disciple, realizes that trusting in God over the things of the world is the necessary and surer step. Jesus' gospel of justice and compassion demands our risking ridicule and cynicism if we are to realize the reign of God in our own time and place. The God who is our lifeline can help us conquer whatever mountains stand in our way and scale whatever chasms threaten our safety. All we have to do is trust enough to make the "commitment move."

Meditation: Is there a "next step" you should take in bridging an estranged relationship or correcting a difficult situation that you are hesitant to "commit" to?

Prayer: God our Redeemer, through baptism we have tied ourselves to you. By your grace, may we have the wisdom and courage to climb your holy mountain. Trusting in your word, may we dare to walk the difficult trail of justice and forgiveness so that we may one day make our way to the place where you dwell forever.

For the Love of God, Let Go!

Readings: Dan 3:25, 34-43; Matt 18:21-35

Scripture:
"So will my heavenly Father do to you,
    unless each of you forgives your brother from your heart."
(Matt 18:35)

Reflection: When you're overcome with anger or resentment at someone, try this exercise: Write down the resentment on a slip of paper. Then make a fist around it and hold it as tightly as you can. Don't let up the pressure. See how long you can hold on to the slip with that intensity. Now try to carry on your day with the paper tightly held in your grip.

After a while, as you can imagine, your fingers will start to ache, your hand will feel paralyzed. With all of your attention and energy focused on maintaining your grip, you'll be distracted from other things you are trying to accomplish. You'll be unable to reach out and touch and feel because your hands are struggling to keep its grasp on this wad of paper.

A silly exercise? Sure. But that is exactly what we allow our spirits and hearts to experience when we let resentments fester, when we let our anger get the best of us, when we steadfastly refuse to forgive or seek forgiveness for whatever wrongs, real or imagined, we have endured or inflicted. Forgiveness is neither easy nor cheap; but forgiveness is the very heart of the Gospel of Jesus—the foundation of the bridges we seek to build to one another, the first brick we pull out of the walls that divide us.

Meditation: Is there some anger or resentment in your life that you struggle to let go of?

Prayer: Loving Father, help us to let go of our angers and resentments, our embarrassments and guilt, and take the first step in repairing our brokenness with others and with you. Help us to transform the dark cold of our winters into the light and warmth of Easter by seeking forgiveness and reconciliation with all who hurt us and whom we have hurt. May your spirit of compassion and forgiveness illuminate our days with your love and peace.

The Road

Readings: Deut 4:1, 5-9; Matt 5:17-19

Scripture:
". . . whoever obeys and teaches these commandments
will be called greatest in the Kingdom of heaven."

(Matt 5:19)

Reflection: Cormac McCarthy's Pulitzer Prize–winning novel
The Road is the dark, compelling story of a father and son
fighting for survival in the midst of nuclear winter.

America has been reduced to ashes. Millions have been
killed; cities and countrysides have been destroyed. The few
people who survived have banded into packs of marauders
robbing and killing for food. A man and his son who managed to survive are making their way from the eternal winter
in the north to the southern coast where, they hope, they will
find warmth and some chance of building a life. The boy,
who was born after the war, has no memory of the better,
happier times his father has known.

Every day of their trek, the father keeps reminding the son
that they are the "good guys" who carry the "fire." The boy
is never quite sure what the fire is—but he believes in the
fire because his father has told him to, and that's good
enough for him. Throughout their journey, the boy displays
compassion for everyone they encounter—even those who
try to kill them for their meager provisions. Along the dark,

gray *Road*, father and son confront starvation, cold, sickness, horror, and death. With the end of their trek in sight, when his father finally succumbs to illness and exhaustion, the boy must take to the *Road* himself, and he begins to understand what the fire is: his father's uncompromising, unconditional love for his son that enabled him to survive.

"Do everything the way we did," his father tells his son, and remember that the fire "is inside you. It was always there. I can see it."

The boy continues on the *Road* with that hope.

Christ calls us, in today's gospel, to pass on the fire—the love of God for all his sons and daughters, the hope of transforming the darkness and bitterness of our world into the kingdom of God, the peace that enables all men and women to live as brothers and sisters in God's Christ. By our commitment to what is right, by our compassion and caring for others, by our ethical and moral convictions, by our sense of awareness and gratitude for all that God has done for us, we do the great work of passing on the fire of the Gospel of compassion and justice.

Meditation: In what ways have you discovered the fire of God's love that enabled you to make your way through a difficulty or challenge you encountered in your own journey along the road?

Prayer: Lord Jesus, inspire us with the fire of your love so that we may, in turn, pass on that fire to others. Bless our efforts to reflect the light and warmth of that fire in our homes and workplaces, our classrooms and playgrounds.

How Wars Really Start

Readings: Jer 7:23-28; Luke 11:14-23

Scripture:
"Every kingdom divided against itself will be laid waste
and house will fall against house." (Luke 11:17)

Reflection: A nine-year-old asks his father, "Dad, how do wars
start?"

"Well, son," his father began, "take World War I. That war
started when Germany invaded Belgium . . ."

"Just a minute," his wife interrupted. "It began when
Archduke Francis Ferdinand of Austria was assassinated by
a Serbian nationalist."

"Well, dear, that was the spark that ignited the fighting,
but the political and economic factors leading to the war had
been in place for some time."

"Yes, I know, honey, but our son asked how the war began
and every history book says that World War I began with
the murder of Archduke Ferdinand of Austria."

Drawing himself up with an air of superiority, the husband
snapped, "Are you answering the question, or am I?"

The wife turned her back on him in a huff, stalked out of
the room and slammed the door behind her.

When the dishes stopped rattling, an uneasy silence fol-
lowed. The nine-year-old then broke the silence: "Dad, you

don't have to say any more about how wars start. I understand now."

Wars begin long before the first shot is fired; households collapse well before the first crack in the foundation; families fall apart days and months and years before the first slammed door. When our own needs come before the common good, when we cannot see or refuse to see things from the perspective of the other person, when the accumulation of wealth and the pursuit of status take the place of the things of God, "war" that destroys the family's unity, the circle of friendship, is inevitable.

Jesus calls us, his disciples of this time and place, to embrace his spirit of reconciliation that compels us to always take the first step in forgiving and being forgiven, his spirit of humility that finds joy in doing good for others, his spirit of compassion that places love before all.

Meditation: How can a change in your attitude or perspective begin to bring peace to a war you are waging in your life?

Prayer: May your love, O Lord, be the foundation of our homes and families; may your forgiveness be the walls that protect our loved ones from the winds and storms that threaten to drive us apart; may your peace be the roof that shields us from the rain and cold; may your compassion be the hearth that warms our hearts all our days.

Redemption on a Crumpled Page

Readings: Hos 14:2-10; Mark 12:28-34

Scripture:
"You shall love the Lord your God with all your heart,
with all your soul,
with all you mind,
and with all your strength . . .
You shall love your neighbor as yourself.
There is no other commandment greater than these."

(Mark 12:29-30, 31)

Reflection: In his acclaimed book *Man's Search for Meaning*, Dr. Viktor Frankl writes of the unspeakable horrors he witnessed as a prisoner in Nazi death camps during World War II. The book is not just a record of Nazi atrocities but a testament of what he learned about the meaning and purpose of life from his experiences and from his fellow prisoners.

When he was arrested, Frankl tried to hide inside his coat a book he had been writing on psychiatry. The manuscript was his life's work. But at Auschwitz, all his possessions and clothes—including his coat—were taken from him, and his manuscript was lost forever.

Frankl writes:

"I had to surrender my clothes and in turn inherited the worn-out rags of an inmate who had been sent to the gas chamber immediately after his arrival at the Auschwitz railway station. Instead of the many pages of my manuscript, I found in the pocket of my newly acquired coat one single page torn out of a Hebrew prayer book, containing the most important Jewish prayer, *Shema Yisrael* [which Jesus cites in today's gospel: *Hear, O Israel! / The Lord our God is Lord alone! / You shall love the Lord your God with all your heart . . .*].

"How could I have interpreted such a 'coincidence' other than as a challenge to suffer bravely. Life has a meaning up to the last moment, and it retains this meaning literally to the end."

In the very act of creating us, God invites us to participate in his act of creation by embracing his Spirit of compassion. It is in our love for one another that humanity most resembles the God in whose image we are formed; it is in charity and selflessness that we live the very life of God. In the two "great commandments" we discover a purpose to our lives much greater and larger than our prejudices, provincialism, and parochialism; in them, we find the ultimate meaning and purpose of the gifts of faith and life.

Meditation: What causes you to hesitate or hold back from loving God and others totally and completely?

Prayer: Father, may we discover purpose and meaning in our lives by loving and honoring each other as your sons and daughters, our brothers and sisters; may we share in your work of creation by re-creating our homes and schools, our workplaces and communities in your justice and peace.

Growing Up

Readings: Hos 6:1-6; Luke 18:9-14

Scripture:
"[F]or everyone who exalts himself will be humbled,
and the one who humbles himself will be exalted."

(Luke 18:14)

Reflection: A newborn child is the center of the world—at least that's the way it seems.

The presence of the newborn monopolizes the life of the entire family. The child's every need and want is provided for. So helpless, so fragile, the infant is doted upon, fussed over, and fretted about by his anxious parents. A baby's tears command the immediate response of Mom and Dad; a baby's laughter is more precious than gold.

But as a child develops and grows and is able to do more and more for himself or herself, the child begins to understand that he or she is not the center of the world, that the world is indeed much bigger than the child's own needs and wants. The child becomes increasingly responsible for his or her own actions and decisions and learns to live with the consequences of those actions and decisions.

As the child enters adulthood, the young adult begins to take on responsibility for the needs and wants of others as well. The older the child becomes, the more removed the child is from "being the center" of things.

The transformation is complete when the once-child-now-adult becomes a parent—and a new child becomes the center of the world.

Thomas Merton wrote that becoming an adult requires that we become humble and recognize that we are not the center of the universe, that other people are not here simply to satisfy our needs and desires. The Gospel of Jesus challenges us to embrace the humble, God-centered faith of the tax collector and not the childish, empty claims of the Pharisee. We manifest our love for God not through self-congratulatory rituals of piety but through heartfelt and sincere love and care for the poor, the needy, the defenseless, the alienated, and the rejected, seeing in them the face of Christ.

Meditation: How can you approach your faith and its practice from a more mature, "adult" perspective? How can your relationship with God be transformed from one of fear of punishment and judgment to one based on gratitude and humility?

Prayer: Father in heaven, help us to "grow up" this Lent, to become adults in our faith. Draw us beyond our own sense of self to realize that the purpose and meaning of this gift of life is found outside of ourselves and beyond our own needs. May we discover the true joy and happiness of life in the compassion we extend and receive from our brothers and sisters.

The Forgiveness Dance

Readings: Josh 5:9a, 10-12; 2 Cor 5:17-21; Luke 15:1-3, 11-32.
The readings for Year A may be used in place of these.

Scripture:
"While [the son] was still a long way off,
his father caught sight of him, and was filled with
compassion.
He ran to his son, embraced him and kissed him.
His son said to him,
'Father, I have sinned . . .'" (Luke 15:20-21)

Reflection: They had one of those fights that keeps married couples honest.

She was shrill, he was insensitive; she railed, he yelled; both said things that cut deeply. Finally, she shut herself off in the kitchen and he stormed downstairs to his workshop.

In their own spaces, each mindlessly fiddled with cookware and tools. As she scrubbed the same pot for several minutes and he oiled every movable part of every power tool he owned, their anger turned to sorrow.

That was a dumb thing to say. She didn't deserve that.

Why did I make such a big deal over nothing?

After a while, he could no longer stand the thought of not loving her or being loved by her. She could no longer bear the dark cloud that hung in the air.

So, he trudged up the stairs to apologize. At the top of the stairs, he opened the door—she was standing right there, on her way to his workshop to say the same thing.

Reconciliation demands that we be willing to be both the prodigal son and the forgiving father. To experience healing forgiveness, we must face up to our culpability and our self-ishness that causes such rifts, as does the son mired in the pigsty—and, given the opportunity, we must be openhearted enough to welcome back into our lives those who hurt us, as does the father who runs (runs!) to meet and embrace his son. Such selfless, unconditional, and complete forgiveness is the cutting edge of the Gospel.

Only in breaking down the walls of estrangement that we erect, only in taking the first step across the divides that have separated us can we dare to call ourselves disciples of Christ. God, before whom all of us are prodigals, calls us to make our homes, parishes, and communities places where we prodigals are always welcomed home by the loving fathers (and mothers) we are all called to be.

Meditation: Is there a situation that could be healed if you offered or sought forgiveness? What is stopping you?

Prayer: Merciful God, make us vessels of your mercy. When we are lost, may your mercy enable us to find our way back; when we are searching for our lost loved ones, may your mercy support us in our anxiety; when we are hurt and angry, may your mercy be a well from which we draw your abundant patience and understanding.

A Mother's Sacrifice

Readings: Isa 65:17-21; John 4:43-54

Scripture:

[T]here was a royal official whose son was ill at Capernaum.
When he heard that Jesus had arrived in Galilee from Judea,
    he went to him and asked him to come down
    and heal his son, who was near death. (John 4:46-47)

Reflection: A monk was traveling through the Himalayas when he encountered a great forest fire. Everyone was trying to fight the raging blaze. The monk noticed a group of villagers looking up into a tree that was about to go up in flames. When the monk asked what they were looking at, they pointed at a nest full of young birds. Above it, the mother bird was circling wildly and calling out warnings to her young ones. There was nothing the bird or the villagers could do, and soon the flames started consuming the branches.

As the nest caught fire, the monk and the onlookers were amazed to see how the mother bird reacted. Instead of flying away from the flames, she flew down and settled on the nest, covering her little ones with her wings. The next moment, she and her nestlings were burned. No one could believe their eyes. The monk then said:

"God created that bird with such love and devotion, that she gave her life trying to protect her young. If her small heart was so full of love, how unfathomable must be the love of her Creator. That is the love that brought him down from heaven to become man. That is the love that made him suffer a painful death for our sake."

Both the mother bird and the royal official of today's gospel are inspirations for those of us who are parents. Both possess the kind of love that God possesses, a love that readily takes on any threat to our children. In his desperate love for his dying child, the official pushes aside all the protocols and stature of his position, including the likely criticism of his superiors and possible repercussions on his career, and seeks out this controversial Jesus, begging him for help. When Jesus tries to put him off, the father will not be deterred: "Please come before my little boy dies." Because of such love, Jesus heals the official's child.

It is the love of this father, the love of the mother bird, that Jesus asks us to embrace: love that transcends boundaries and stereotypes; love that triumphs over fear; love that seeks healing and restoration above all else; love that recognizes every man, woman, and child as children of God and brothers and sisters to each one of us.

Meditation: Have you ever been surprised by what your own love for another enabled you to do?

Prayer: Heavenly Father, breathe again your Parent's love into our hearts and spirits. Open our hearts to love regardless of our fears, regardless of the consequences, regardless of the costs. In imitating Jesus' example, may we heal our world in your peace and restore it in your justice.

A Strange Question

Readings: Ezek 47:1-9, 12; John 5:1-16

Scripture: "Do you want to be well?" (John 5:6)

Reflection: What a strange question Jesus asks the sick man struggling to wash in the healing waters of Bethesda: "Do you want to be well?"

Well, of course, Jesus! I've been flat on my back for thirty-eight years! But there's no one to plunge me into the pool. By the time I get there someone takes my place in line . . .

Then Jesus says to the man—orders the man—"Rise, take up your mat, and walk."

And the man picks up his mat and walks.

But the question Jesus asks at the beginning of their encounter is not as strange as it sounds. Truth be told, we often are not as interested in being *healed* as we are in simply *feeling better*. As long as we can justify in our own minds why things are not as they should be, if we can rationalize our failure or refusal to do what is right, if we can convince ourselves and others that everything is really alright . . . we're fine, we're okay, we're good with it.

But we are not "well"—we are not healed.

To be healed means, first, recognizing our *need* for healing and wanting it badly enough to "stand up" and stop feeling sorry for ourselves, to "pick up our mat" and put away the rationalizations and excuses, to "walk" the difficult path that brings healing to our hearts and spirits—the path of forgiveness, compassion, humility, mercy, justice.

This season of Lent confronts us with our need to be *healed*—not just made to feel better for the moment. Christ comes to make us well—complete and whole in the life and love of God.

Meditation: Is there a painful or distressing situation in your life that could be healed by your willingness to change?

Prayer: Christ Jesus, as you healed the sick man at Bethesda, heal us of our fears, our disappointments, our estrangements, our despair. Give us the courage to stand up and shake off the worries and burdens that weigh us down; give us the vision that enables us to pick up our mats of sadness and despair and to realize your life and love around us; give us the grace to walk in the light of your peace so that, this Lent, we may truly be healed of the blindness of our hearts and the illness of our souls.

My Monastery Is a Minivan

Readings: Isa 49:8-15; John 5:17-30

Scripture:
"[T]he Father loves the Son
  and shows him everything that he himself does,
  and he will show him greater works that these,
  so that you may be amazed." (John 5:20)

Reflection: When asked our religion, most of us would describe ourselves as "Catholic" or "Christian," but we would tend to back away from daring to call ourselves "disciple" or "follower." That description rightly belongs to the great heroes of our faith: the apostles and holy men and women of the gospel, the saints and martyrs, the Francises of Assisi, the Mother Teresas, the Dorothy Days, the Albert Schweitzers. Our lives are too ordinary, our professions too worldly to dare imagine that we are doing the work of the gospel Jesus.

But Denise Roy has found that in her life as a wife and mother she has been doing exactly what Jesus did. She writes in her book *My Monastery Is a Minivan: Where the Daily Is Divine and the Routine Becomes Prayer*:

"For two decades, I have broken bread, poured grape juice, preached, prayed, told stories, bestowed blessings, taken care of the sick, heard confessions. I have been a parent. These have been the sacraments of my daily life and, I suspect, of yours. These are simple, sacred acts. These are how we mediate love, as we minister to our own little congregations—children, spouse, family, and friends."

At one time in her life, Ms. Roy, who is also a psychotherapist and spiritual director, wanted to be a contemplative nun—but her family's minivan has become her monastery where she prays and meditates and transports angels from one location to another.

"If we pay attention, any moment or any place or any person might be a bearer of wisdom," she observes. "Nothing is off-limits as a potential source of wisdom, as the dwelling place for divinity."

Jesus' invitation in the gospel to fishermen, tax collectors, farmers, laborers, and peasants to be his followers is extended to us as well, here in our own time and place. Our baptisms were our acceptances of that invitation to take on the work of discipleship in the homes and classrooms and workplaces and minivans where we live our lives. Christ invites us to take on the same work that was entrusted to him by the Father: to bring others to God through the Gospel of peace, reconciliation, and love.

Meditation: What common, simple, everyday activity or task of yours can you make into a work of God?

Prayer: Father, open our minds and hearts to be the Word of your Son. Help us to give voice to that Word not only in our churches but in our homes, our classrooms, our work spaces, and gathering places.

The New Moses, the Second Passover

Readings: Exod 32:7-14; John 5:31-47

Scripture:
"Do not think that I will accuse you before the Father:
    the one who will accuse you is Moses,
    in whom you have placed your hope.
For if you had believed Moses,
    you would have believed me,
    because he wrote about me." (John 5:45-46)

Reflection: This year, as the Christian world observes Holy Week, our Jewish neighbors will celebrate Passover. At their family tables they will remember the seminal event in their history: the night when Moses and Aaron and their ancestors began their long exodus from slavery to freedom in the land given them by God.

Moses continues to be the most revered figure in Judaism. He led the Israelites on their forty-year sojourn through the desert to the Promised Land. He was the lawgiver and judge who established the moral and ethical code on which the nation of Israel was established. He was the prophet and mediator between God and God's beloved.

At the Easter Vigil, we will relive the exodus event in Word and sacrament. With Moses and his tribes, we will walk through the waters of the Red Sea to a new identity as the people of God. With Christ, we will rise from the waters of baptism to the life of the Risen One. We will break the bread of the New Passover with the Risen Christ, the lamb sacrificed for us.

In today's gospel, Jesus identifies his Messiahship with the work of Moses. Jesus comes not to destroy or supplant what Moses began in the Sinai but to continue and complete it in his own passover from life to death. In Christ, God calls us to a second exodus from the slavery of sin and death to the freedom of selfless servanthood. In Christ, the law given to Moses on Sinai is perfected and completed in the Gospel of compassion and forgiveness. In Christ, God becomes one of us in the complexities and struggles of being human.

For both Jews and Christians, Passover is a solemn memorial of freedom and liberation. The celebration marks a nation's freedom from slavery to nationhood and a people's liberation from the destruction of sin to the possibilities of God's Spirit dwelling in our midst. The work of establishing God's reign begun by Moses and continued in Christ now becomes, in our own passover in the waters of baptism, our work and call.

Meditation: From what attitudes, situations, and challenges do you seek liberation this Easter? What first steps must you take in this exodus?

Prayer: God of all holiness, you raised up Moses as your prophet and lawgiver; by living your Word of love may we break the chains of sin that shackle us. You raised up your beloved Son Jesus from the grave to the new life of Easter: may we rise with him from our tombs of hopelessness and despair to the hope of his resurrection.

March 19:
Saint Joseph, Husband of the Blessed Virgin Mary

A Parent's Dreams

Readings: 2 Sam 7:4-5a, 12-14a, 16; Rom 4:13, 16-18, 22;
Matt 1:16, 18-21, 24a or Luke 2:41-51a

Scripture:
[T]he angel of the Lord appeared to [Joseph] in a dream
   and said,
"Joseph, son of David,
do not be afraid to take Mary your wife into your home.
For it is through the Holy Spirit
   that this child has been conceived in her." (Matt 1:20)

Reflection: From the moment a couple learns they will be
parents, they begin to dream about and for their child. The
first dreams are for a safe birth, a strong and complete body,
good health and physical development. Then parents dream
that their son or daughter will excel in sports, master the
sciences, distinguish themselves in the arts and literature.
They may dare to dream that their child may one day be
elected president, become the quarterback for the Cowboys,
sing at the Met, or discover the cure for cancer.

Along the way, of course, the dreams change. Where they
once dreamed about the Nobel Prize, mom and dad will now
settle for passing math. The dream of a World Series ring is
overshadowed by the anguished prayer that their son will
walk again or that their daughter will wake up after a

horrible accident. The dream of a Bill Gates-like fortune disappears when the prayer becomes a desperate plea for the child's safe return from a dangerous sojourn into the world of drugs, sex, and violence.

Like any parent, St. Joseph, whose feast we celebrate today, had hopes and dreams for his family, as well. Two of his "dreams" are recorded in the Gospel of Matthew. In today's gospel, the angel assures Joseph that he should not fear about taking his beloved Mary as his wife despite her pregnancy, that his compassion and love for her will not be disappointed. After Jesus' birth, when King Herod begins his murderous search for the child, Joseph is instructed by an angel in a dream to take his family to the safety of Egypt.

Fear, disappointment, adversity, and tragedy will change our more grandiose dreams for our children. But, as Joseph learns from his dreams, the most important things we can dream for our children are the love and safety of family, the acceptance and forgiveness of understanding parents, the knowledge and wisdom of the God of graciousness and peace.

Meditation: What are the most important and lasting things that parents can dream for their sons and daughters?

Prayer: God our Father, you dream for us to live in your love and peace until we come to your dwelling place in heaven. Help us to imitate the compassion and humility of Joseph that we may work to make that dream a reality for our children, for our families, and for ourselves.

Patron Saint of Seekers

Readings: Jer 11:18-20; John 7:40-53

Scripture:
Nicodemus, one of their members who had come to [Jesus]
     earlier, said to them,
   "Does our law condemn a man before it first hears him
   and finds out what he is doing?" (John 7:50-51)

Reflection: Today's gospel is one of three appearances of the
Pharisee Nicodemus in John's gospel.

Nicodemus was a member of the Jewish ruling class. John
identifies him as one of a small group of Jewish elite who
are favorably disposed toward Jesus, even though they do
not completely understand him or his teachings. In John 3,
Nicodemus arranges to meet Jesus secretly and asks questions
about Jesus' mission as Messiah. It is during this encounter
that we hear the revelation, "God so loved the world that he
gave his only Son." Nicodemus tells no one of their meeting.

Today's gospel is Nicodemus's second appearance. The
plot to do away with Jesus is taking shape. In the course of
the debate, Nicodemus defends Jesus, arguing that it is
against the holy law to condemn Jesus before a hearing.
Nicodemus is ridiculed by the council for his position.

Nicodemus is often portrayed as a coward, skulking
around Jesus at night or when Jesus is dead; he plays it safe,

avoiding commitments and entanglements that might place him on the "wrong" side. His training as a Pharisee has limited his outlook to a narrow, literal interpretation of his religion and the law. But Jesus welcomes him as a sincere seeker of God. Jesus understands that Nicodemus is wrestling with the narrow, insular view of the truth he has learned and Jesus' more liberating and complete wisdom that is well outside his comfort zone. Nicodemus's surprising and brave defense of Jesus in today's gospel is a clear indication that Jesus' teaching has opened up something inside Nicodemus. He has begun to understand the Savior's baptism of death and resurrection.

Like Nicodemus, we struggle to make sense of Jesus; we wrestle with reconciling his Gospel with the complexities of our world. Jesus neither rejects us nor ridicules us but walks with us in our moving back and forth between what is safe and familiar and the new but demanding love of God.

Like Nicodemus, we are all seekers, and Christ has assured us of his company on our journey.

Meditation: What one teaching of Jesus do you struggle the most to understand and embrace in your life?

Prayer: Christ Jesus, be our courage and our strength as we cope with the obstacles that isolate us from you. Walk with us as we struggle to become your disciples and live lives worthy of our identity as sons and daughters of the Father and brothers and sisters to one another in you.

From Pretty to Pretentious in Three Days

Readings: Isa 43:16-21; Phil 3:8-14; John 8:1-11. The readings from Year A may be used in place of these.

Scripture:
"Let the one among you who is without sin
be the first to throw a stone at her." (John 8:7)

Reflection: The fifth-grader came home from school bubbling with excitement after being voted "Prettiest Girl in Class."

She was even more excited when she came home the next day after the class had voted her "Most Popular."

But a few days later she was considerably less excited when she had announced to her Mom that she had won a third contest.

"What were you voted this time?" her mother asked.

"Most Stuck-Up," the girl cried.

These days of Lent are a call both to accept our gifts and abilities and to acknowledge our sinfulness and culpability for our failure to live the Gospel we profess to believe and to recognize our need for redemption and resurrection. Confronting the demons of the world must begin with confronting the demons within our own hearts.

That is Jesus' challenge to the scribes and Pharisees who demand judgment against the adulteress: we cannot change what is beyond us until we change what is within us; we cannot lift up the fallen until we realize that we have fallen; we cannot raise others to health and hope until we seek our own healing; we cannot pass sentence on others until we judge our own lives.

The Pharisees and scribes' approach to morality does have a certain appeal: just eliminate the problem. But Jesus challenges them to a more lasting, permanent conversion: "Put down your stones of indignation and anger and look to your hearts, to that place within every one of us where good and evil meet. Understand the disappointments, the despair, the selfishness that drive you to sin. Realize the hurt, the pain, the destruction others suffer because of your sin. Put aside your rationalizations and excuses and embrace the love and mercy of God, who knows our hearts better than we do ourselves."

Meditation: In what ways do you sense sin getting the upper hand in your attitudes and decision making?

Prayer: Father of forgiveness, make us a people of compassion. Give us the courage to reach out to those who fall along the road we all travel so that we may transform what is evil into the reflection of your love. Humble us with the grace to seek forgiveness when we fall so that we may replace the hurt we have caused with healing and reconciliation.

March 22: Monday of the Fifth Week of Lent

Learning from Powerlessness

Readings: Dan 13:1-9, 15-17, 19-30, 33-62 or 13:41c-62; John 8:12-20

Scripture:
"I am the light of the world.
Whoever follows me will not walk in darkness,
    but will have the light of life." (John 8:12)

Reflection: In her recent book *An Altar in the World: A Geography of Faith*, Barbara Brown Taylor recalls a four-day power outage at her farm in the middle of winter.

While the first day was one of joyful quiet, by day two Taylor and her husband were busy splitting logs, refilling kerosene heaters, and keeping the animals' water supplies unfrozen. There was a refrigerator full of spoiling food to be dealt with and an ancient generator to be poked and prodded in hopes of restoring it to service.

By the third day, Taylor "dreaded the setting of the sun, when everything got colder and harder to do. . . . Everywhere I turned, the darkness exposed my helplessness. I could not watch a movie, could not work on my computer, could not do laundry, could not take a bath, could not even walk across the room without fear of bashing my shin. I had lost power. I was without power. I had no power."

When the power was finally restored on the fourth day, Taylor writes, she had a new appreciation for such phrases as "the power of God" and the "light of Christ."

"A power outage [makes] a great spiritual practice. . . . Live as most people in the world live, preoccupied with survival. . . . Long for the light you cannot procure for yourself, and feel your heart swell with gratitude—every single morning—when the sun comes up. Value warmth. Prize shelter. Praise the miracle of flowing water."

Barbara Brown Taylor's experience coping with a winter power outage offers an insight for all of us as we struggle this Lent to turn away from the trivial and meaningless in order to embrace the "powerful" things of God. The gospel Jesus comes as the light of God that dispels the darkness of our lives and illuminates our journey to the kingdom of the Father. In his light, we realize our own powerlessness and embrace the energy of grace to sustain us as we seek God's compassion and justice in the everyday and the ordinary.

Meditation: What lessons of humility and gratitude did you learn the last time you suffered cold and discomfort due to helplessness?

Prayer: Christ our light, shatter the darkness of sin and selfishness that shroud our lives; warm the winter cold of estrangement, anger, and distrust. Give us the courage and grace to see with your eyes, that we may recognize your presence in every person and moment, and to discern your wisdom in all things.

The Scourge of God

Readings: Num 21:4-9, John 8:21-30

Scripture:
He said to them, "You belong to what is below,
  I belong to what is above.
You belong to this world,
but I do not belong to this world." (John 8:23)

Reflection: A band of marauding tribesmen descended on a small village. Every one of the villagers, including a small community of monks, fled into the mountains—except one monk who refused to abandon the monastery.

The outlaw chief burst through the monastery gate to find the old monk praying in the garden. Enraged that the old man refused to cower in his presence, the chief thundered, "Do you know who I am? I am he who can run you through with a sword without batting an eyelash."

The monk looked at the commander with a calm and patient look. "And do you know who I am? I am he who can let you run me through with a sword without batting an eyelash."

The ways and values of God often challenge what society considers strong, profitable, and useful. Frankly, God's sense of generosity, love, and forgiveness strikes us with an extravagance that offends our own sense of fair play. But trusting in the things of God frees us from what our scales, clocks, and computer printouts determine is fair and profitable, enabling us to re-create and transform our world in the goodness and mercy of God. The Christ of Lent and Easter calls us to realize our humbleness before God, who enables us to do extraordinary things for one another. In taking on the spirit of compassion, forgiveness, and mercy that is of "above," we can transform our world "below" in the joy and hope of Easter.

Meditation: What values of God—things of "above"—do you find yourself appreciating more and more as you struggle in the world here "below"?

Prayer: Lord God, help us to appreciate the things of "above" and not be satisfied with the things of "below." Transform our attitudes, enlighten our vision, instill in us your wisdom to seek you and your way of holiness and peace in all things.

Real Guts

Readings: Dan 3:14-20, 91-92, 95; John 8:31-42

Scripture:
"If you remain in my word, you will truly be my disciples,
and you will know the truth, and the truth will set you
free." (John 8:31-32)

Reflection: Top brass from the Army, Navy, and Marine
Corps were arguing about which branch of the military had
the bravest troops. They decided to settle the dispute using
an enlisted man from each service.

The army general called a private over and ordered him
to climb to the top of the base flagpole while singing "The
Caissons Go Rolling Along," then let go with both hands,
and salute. The private quickly complied.

Next, the admiral ordered a soldier to climb the pole,
polish the brass knob at the top, sing "Anchors Aweigh,"
salute smartly, and jump off. The sailor did as he was told
and plummeted to the concrete.

Finally, the marine general called over a young marine.
He was ordered to do exactly as the army and navy men had
done, but in full battle gear, pack filled with bricks, loaded
weapon held high. The marine took one look at the com-
mandant and said, "You're out of your mind, sir."

The marine commander turned to the other officers and
smiled. "Now, gentlemen, that's guts!"

At some point in our lives, if we are to live a life with any sense of purpose and meaning, we have to confront exactly what we believe—and be willing to pay whatever price for that belief, for that concept of "truth" we hold dear. To walk away, to duck the question, to sacrifice the values we hold in our hearts out of fear for the sake of our career, our reputation, or our safety is to render ourselves and our lives shallow and meaningless.

Christ calls us and all who would be his disciples to embrace his Gospel with not just a mumbled, rote yes on our lips but with the honesty and integrity of the human heart. To be sure, such authentic truth can be challenging and back-breaking; truth can make us squirm and feel uncomfortable; truth can demand from us a response that is humiliating and costly.

But our response to such truth is everything.

Meditation: What has been the most difficult truth or reality you have had to deal with? How has accepting that truth changed the way you dealt with that situation?

Prayer: God of wisdom, open our eyes to recognize you and your truth in all things. Open our hearts to accept what is good and just, despite the costs. Open our spirits to know the freedom and joy that is ours in embracing your Spirit of truth, mercy, and compassion.

The Season of "Annunciation"

Readings: Isa 7:10-14; 8:10; Heb 10:4-10; Luke 1:26-38

Scripture:
"Behold, I am the handmaid of the Lord.
May it be done to me according to your word." (Luke 1:38)

Reflection: It takes less than a minute to read Luke's account of the annunciation. And that's how long we tend to think it took: Mary is praying (at least that's what all the paintings indicate) and Gabriel appears. The angel greets Mary, outlines the plan, Mary asks a few questions, Gabriel says, "Not to worry," Mary gives her consent, and Gabriel disappears. On to Elizabeth's house.

But how could it happen so quickly?

A young girl suddenly finds herself pregnant. She is confused and terrified. She has to face her fiancé and family. Her world has been turned upside down. She faces ostracism, rejection—and, by the letter of the law, worse.

With the help of Gabriel, Mary tries to make sense of what is about to happen. The questions and doubts come over time. Gabriel becomes the sacred presence that enables her faith to develop, her trust to take root, her direction to be made clear. The annunciation may very well have taken place over hours, days, perhaps weeks. It may have included a painful confrontation with Joseph and the wise counsel of her own parents and Elizabeth. But the Spirit of God is present to her to help her and Joseph transform this difficult situation into life, this scandal into grace.

And, in the end, Mary gives her ascent.

Fiat.

Let it be done to me.

Mary's experience mirrors our own. Discerning God's will demands time and thoughtfulness. In God's annunciations to us, we have a great deal to process, to sort out, to make sense of. Today's solemnity of the Annunciation—nine months before Christmas—is the perfect Marian feast for Lent, these forty days when our hearts and spirits are especially opened to the presence of Gabriel announcing to us that the Lord is with us, that we have nothing to fear, that we have been called by God to bring his Christ into our own time and place.

And God gives us these days to sort it all out, to make sense of it, so that we can say with Mary, *Fiat*—"Let it be done."

Meditation: Is there some decision or issue you are currently dealing with in which you are finding it difficult to say yes to what would be the right thing to do? What is causing you to hesitate to place your trust in the call of God?

Prayer: Gracious God, may we possess the faith and trust of your daughter Mary to say yes to your calling us to make your presence known in our time and place. May this Lenten season be a time for discerning your annunciations to us to bring your Son into our own homes and hearts.

Game On

Readings: Jer 20:10-13; John 10:31-42

Scripture:
"If I do not perform my Father's works, do not believe me;
  but if I perform them, even if you do not believe me,
  believe the works, so that you may realize and under-
    stand
  that the Father is in me and I am in the Father."

(John 10:37-38)

Reflection: When Michelle Robinson was getting serious about the young lawyer she was dating, she asked her older brother Craig to "vet" her suitor.

So Craig, a former basketball star and now head coach, took the lanky attorney with the large ears to play some ball. After a few hours on the court, Craig was impressed: this guy made the most of the skills he had, but he was no ball hog—he willingly passed and blocked as necessary for his team to score. Craig saw integrity, leadership, discipline, and self-respect in Michelle's suitor in the way he approached the game and the way he treated his teammates.

Yeah, Craig reported back to his sister, this Barack Obama was okay.

We can all talk a good game—but there comes the time in everyone's life when we have to take the ball and play. Our faith, our sense of justice, our moral and ethical integrity find their true worth in our actual "play" and show what we have in the effort we exert, in our total giving of what we have, in our ability to work for the common good. In the view of Craig Robinson, the way you play the game indicates the values you live in your life; the approach you take to your teammates is the true indicator of your commitment to what is right and just.

In today's confrontation with an angry group of Jews, Jesus asks that they look only at the works he has performed. Jesus seeks to reveal the love of the Father in doing the Father's works. "Never mind what you have heard," Jesus urges them. "Watch my moves; see what I do."

Lent challenges us to assess the integrity and commitment of our own work of justice, forgiveness, and compassion.

Meditation: What are your best "moves" in terms of being a disciple of Jesus, and what areas of your "game" in living the Gospel need work?

Prayer: Christ Jesus, may every moment of our lives reflect our baptism into your death and resurrection. Give us the generosity of heart to recognize those chances to bring your love into the life of another; give us the humility of spirit to get beyond our own needs and fears to try to do for others what you would do; give us the courage of faith to remember that in our kindness and love we can remake our lives and world into your kingdom.

The Caiaphas Syndrome

Readings: Ezek 37:21-28; John 11:45-56

Scripture:
[S]ince [Caiaphas] was high priest for that year,
he prophesied that Jesus was going to die for the nation,
and not only for the nation,
but also to gather into one the dispersed children of God.
So from that day on they planned to kill him. (John 11:51-52)

Reflection: In the gospel accounts of Jesus' passion, we encounter humanity at its worst. We witness not only the cruelty humans are capable of inflicting on one another but humankind's uncanny ability to twist events and manipulate the facts to justify such evil.

Caiaphas is a case in point. He is the high priest at the time of Jesus' trial and, as such, he would preside at the proceedings. Although the office of high priest was controlled by the aristocratic families from Jerusalem, the occupant held office only as long as he enjoyed Roman favor. Caiaphas's eighteen-year tenure as chief priest testifies to his political shrewdness and savvy.

In today's gospel, the leaders of the Jewish community are meeting to deal with the "Jesus problem." The popularity of this itinerant rabbi could be disastrous for the Jewish community—and their leaders. The Romans do not take kindly to self-proclaimed messiahs whose popularity among the people begins to unsettle the peace and order of their rule.

The unscrupulous and arrogant Caiaphas is determined to get rid of this Jesus who threatens the chief priest's comfortable, self-serving "order." The justice of the sentence is of no concern to Caiaphas. Caiaphas rationalizes that the death of Jesus will be for the good of the nation, that it will be a means of uniting "the dispersed children of God."

Caiaphas's prophecy becomes Jesus' death sentence.

And yet, despite the anger and deceit behind his words and the travesty of justice that the Sanhedrin will carry out, the evangelist John describes them as a "prophecy." The high priest strikingly expresses the meaning of the sufferings of God's Christ: that God will act in the death of Jesus to bring his "children" together in the light of the resurrection.

Sometimes we use God and faith as the means to an end that is anything but faith-filled. We invoke God to judge and condemn. God has given us the gift of faith not to be Caiaphas-like agents of judgment and destruction but Christ-like vehicles of compassion and justice.

Meditation: In what ways do we treat the gospel Jesus as a problem and seek a Caiaphas-like rationalization to justify our un-Christlike behavior?

Prayer: God of forgiveness, help us to be the means of resurrection rather than agents of death. May our faithfulness to your Son's Gospel compel us to seek your love in every relationship, your forgiveness in every crisis, your justice in every trial.

"Cloak" Sunday

Readings: Luke 19:28-40; Isa 50:4-7; Phil 2:6-11; Luke 22:14–23:56 or 23:1-49

Scripture:
[They] threw their cloaks over the colt,
and helped Jesus to mount.
As he rode along,
the people were spreading their cloaks on the road.

(Luke 19:35-36)

Reflection: Notice something missing in Luke's version of Jesus' entry into Jerusalem on Palm Sunday?

No palm branches.

Unlike the other three gospel accounts, Luke makes no mention of palm fronds being waved or hosannas being sung. Instead, the crowds repeat the song of the angels at Bethlehem welcoming the newborn king—"Peace in heaven / and glory in the highest"—that Luke records at the beginning of his gospel story.

In Luke's account of Palm Sunday, the people place their single most important article of clothing—their cloaks—along Jesus' path. A cloak was the most expensive garment they possessed. Most people owned only one cloak that was constantly mended, never discarded. For the poorest of the poor, a cloak was more than an article of clothing: it was their shelter and home. The holy poor of Luke's narrative place all that they have at the disposal of the Messiah-king.

The Sunday of the Lord's Passion is about emptying oneself in order to be filled with the love of God. As Christ empties himself of his very divinity so that humanity might be reconciled with God, the people of Jerusalem empty themselves of their most precious possession to welcome into their midst the Anointed One of God and his reign of peace. To be disciples of the Messiah Jesus is to put aside our "cloaks" of comfort and self-absorption to embrace Christ's spirit of humility and selflessness, to empty ourselves of our pride and our own wants and needs in order to become vessels of God's life and love.

Meditation: What is your "cloak" made of that you might take off and place before the Messiah to enter the Jerusalem of your own heart?

Prayer: Christ our Redeemer, may we not only remember your passion, death, and resurrection this Holy Week, but may we enter, heart and soul, into your passover from death to life. Let the example of your selfless compassion guide our faltering steps as we struggle to follow you from Jerusalem to the upper room, from agony to trial, from crucifixion to burial. Help us to empty ourselves of our own hurts and wants in order to become vessels of your mercy and consolation for others. May we take up our crosses as you took up yours in the certain hope that our experiences of crucifixion for the sake of justice and integrity may be transformed into the vindication of Easter.

March 29: Monday of Holy Week

The "Scent" of Generosity

Readings: Isa 42:1-7; John 12:1-11

Scripture:
Mary took a liter of costly perfumed oil
  made from genuine aromatic nard
  and anointed the feet of Jesus and dried them with her
    hair;
  the house was filled with the fragrance of the oil.

(John 12:3)

Reflection: It seems a little extravagant, if not ostentatious, to some of the guests at the party, but Mary, the quiet sister of Lazarus and Martha, welcomes Jesus the best way she knows. One can only imagine the depth of her gratitude for what Jesus had done for her little family in bringing back her brother from the grave. She takes a small jar of expensive oil (probably costing all she had), breaks the clay container, and gently anoints the feet of Jesus. The whole house "was filled with the fragrance of the oil," the evangelist John writes.

But in breaking the jar, Mary fills the house with much more than the beautiful aroma of perfume. Mary's simple act of welcome fills the house with love. Her generosity instills a spirit of understanding and compassion among the guests. Judas's transparent attempt to diminish her is deflected by Jesus, underscoring the effect her gift has had on the household.

Broken as an act of welcome to her beloved friend, Mary's small jar of spices is an example to all of us of the "fragrance" of joy and peace, of comfort and care with which we can fill our own houses when we break open our own vessels for the sake of those we love.

Meditation: What act of selflessness can you break open to bring peace and joy to your own family or community?

Prayer: Father, in his selfless and humble emptying of himself for us, your Son transformed our lives from despair to hope, from pain to wholeness, from sadness to joy, from death to life. May we empty ourselves of selfishness and artifice to become vessels of your grace and forgiveness; may we break open our jars of compassion and generosity to fill our homes and communities with your peace and healing.

Idealism Lost

Readings: Isa 49:1-6; John 13:21-33, 36-38

Scripture:
Jesus said to [Judas], "What you are going to do,
    do quickly." . . .
Jesus answered [Peter], . . .
"Amen, amen, I say to you, the cock will not crow
  before you deny me three times." (John 13:27, 38)

Reflection: They were both part of Jesus' group of twelve.

One was an idealist. He found the charismatic Jesus a compelling leader and his message one of extraordinary hope and vision. Establishing the kingdom of God in the here and now was enormously appealing to such a young, enthusiastic zealot. But as the months stretched into years, he lost his idealism—or he grew impatient with the lack of practical progress Jesus was making. Shouldn't Jesus be using his considerable gifts to take on the established order and entrenched leadership to create the new kingdom he kept talking about? Prayers and piety are one thing, but this was the time for action. Over time, his unrealized hopes brought him disappointment, sadness, frustration, anger, and bitterness.

Judas the idealist had become Judas the cynic.

The other was the headstrong leader of the group. Whatever the issue, he charged ahead. He would ask the hard questions and was willing to say what was on everyone's mind. He often served as Jesus' foil. He was the only one of the Twelve to say it: "You are the Messiah" (Matt 16:16). Later, when some were abandoning Jesus because of some hard sayings, Peter remained steadfast: "Master, to whom shall we go? You have the words of eternal life" (John 6:68). But then Jesus the Wonder-Worker, the Rabbi, the Beloved of God, became Jesus the Accused, the Condemned, the Crucified.

Peter's hope was trumped by fear. At the sound of the crowing cock, Peter had to face the sad reality that his beliefs did not match his words.

The stories of Judas and Peter are stories of enthusiasm that fade over time, hope that deteriorates in the wake of constant disappointment, idealism that shatters in the face of hard reality. Both men are unable to understand that the journey to Easter is by way of the cross.

Their experience in the Holy Week gospel is not unlike ours. To experience the new life of the Easter Christ demands our passing over with him from the death of self to the re-creating of the heart in the compassion of God.

Meditation: What beliefs or principles have you lost faith in or have you become cynical about?

Prayer: Gracious God, do not let us lose hope in the possibilities of your compassion and mercy in our own time and place. May your grace sustain our hope in your life conquering death, your spirit of reconciliation healing estrangement, your justice reigning over all peoples and nations.

The Going Rate

Readings: Isa 50:4-9a; Matt 26:14-25

Scripture:
[The chief priests] paid [Judas] thirty pieces of silver,
and from that time on he looked for an opportunity to
hand him over. (Matt 26:15b-16)

Reflection: *Thirty pieces of silver.*

It is one of the coldest phrases in the gospel.

That Judas, one of Jesus' most trusted friends, would sell him into death for thirty pieces of silver sickens us. Such greed, such callousness, such evil numbs us.

Thirty pieces of silver—the price for doing away with Jesus.

But in our own lives, we do away with Jesus for even lesser amounts. We sell off God and the things of God for far less.

We sell time with our families for a few extra dollars in overtime, for a promotion, for professional affirmation.

We sell those marked as geeks and nerds into abuse and ridicule in order to protect our own false superiority.

We sell the poor into an eternal prison of poverty rather than part with a few pieces of our own silver.

We sell off our relationship with God for anything that is more profitable or more fun.

True, we're nowhere near as evil or as callous as Judas— but we have, at some time, collected our thirty pieces of silver.

Meditation: Who or what have you sold for the sake of your own safety, self-preservation, or gain?

Prayer: Loving God, open our hearts to let go of the silver we stubbornly and greedily cling to. In this season of Easter transformation, refocus our vision in order to see you in every moment of our lives; re-center our spirits in your love that we may treasure the love of family and friends before all else and look forward to bringing your love into the lives of the poor, the lost, and the hopeless among us.

April 1: Holy Thursday (Maundy Thursday)

Becoming the Caregiver

Readings: Exod 12:1-8, 11-14; 1 Cor 11:23-26; John 13:1-15

Scripture:
"If I, therefore, the master and teacher, have washed your
    feet,
    you ought to wash one another's feet.
I have given you a model to follow,
    so that as I have done for you, you should also do."

(John 13:14-15)

Reflection: At first, she refused to believe the doctor's diagnosis. She resolved to carry on as if nothing was wrong, but she soon conceded that the cancer was destroying her strength and energy. She cried for days and closed herself off from others. She was angry at God, the doctors, everyone.

She eventually found the courage to accept what was happening and the faith to place her life in God's hands.

That's when the transformation took place—she who could do so little for herself physically became the caregiver of others. Those who cared for her were buoyed by her faith and her sense of peace; they felt a new pride and sense of purpose in their work because of her support. Those who came to cheer her up found themselves lifted up by her serenity and optimism. She became a wellspring of love and peace for her family and friends. Although there were difficult days, her generosity of spirit transformed her illness into an occasion of grace. She embraced the spirit of the *Mandatum*. She became a footwasher in the spirit of Jesus.

In his last "parable" to his friends, the final teaching that would be his legacy, Jesus calls all of us who would be his disciples to put aside our cloaks of pride, of fear, of self, and take up the towel and basin of the footwasher. To put aside our own needs and hurts and make the needs and hurts of others our own is to see our lives in the light of Jesus' selfless compassion; to wash the foot of another person requires Christ's spirit of humility and generosity, of respect and love for the other person; to allow another to wash our feet requires us to trust, to let go of our compulsion to be in control, to acknowledge our need to be healed and forgiven.

It is only when we become authentic footwashers that we will become the church of the Eucharist and witnesses of the resurrection that Jesus calls us to become tonight.

Meditation: In what ways can you wash the feet of another in the spirit of Jesus' humility and compassion?

Prayer: Gracious Father, tonight we remember the beginning of Jesus' passover. May we humbly and joyfully wash the feet of one another and allow others to wash our feet in their acts of kindness and forgiveness. As we receive this night the bread and wine of the Eucharist, may we become Christ's body and blood for our broken, hurting world.

Preparation Day

Readings: Isa 52:13–53:12; Heb 4:14-16; 5:7-9; John 18:1–19:42

Scripture:
It was preparation day for Passover, and it was about noon.
(John 19:14)

Reflection: It was a very busy day, the day before a major holiday. There was shopping to be done and there were dinner preparations to complete. The house needed to be cleaned and guests needed to be welcomed. Merchants had customers to serve and transactions to complete before the start of the holiday at sunset.

In his account of Jesus' passion, John notes that it was the preparation day before the Sabbath, and that year the Passover feast began on the Sabbath. Everyone was too busy to notice what was taking place in "official" Jerusalem. In John's passion narrative, there are no taunting crowds demanding Jesus' blood. Jesus' arrest and trial, taking place in the middle of the night, are handled by Pilate, his soldiers, and the Jewish authorities. So few people witness Jesus' death that John identifies them by name.

Some Scripture scholars believe that John's account is the most accurate description of what actually happened on Good Friday. The depiction of massive crowds clamoring for Jesus' death in the other three gospels was probably not the case—Pilate and his forces would not have countenanced such a public spectacle. To them, the Jesus "incident" was a Jewish matter that concerned them only insofar as it could disturb public order. Pilate and company took care of it as they would any other the problem—with immediate, cold, mercilous efficiency. So while Jerusalem went about the business of Passover, God was putting into motion a second passover.

As a brisk trade in the buying and selling of lambs for Passover was taking place all over the city, the Lamb of God was slain just outside the gates. The new passover was completed on a cross planted on a hill. God was calling his people to a new exodus from death to life.

This Good Friday is also a day of preparation. The events of this day are not an end in themselves but the means to a much greater event: God completes the work of his second genesis by re-creating humanity in the paschal mystery.

On this busy spring Good Friday, God transforms humanity to its very core.

And humanity seems too busy to notice.

Meditation: Is there something special you might do to remember the crucified Jesus this Good Friday?

Prayer: Compassionate God, we stand before the cross humbled by your love, chastened by the injustice and hatred that brought your Son to it. May Jesus' cross re-create us in your compassion and forgiveness; may his Gospel lead us in our exodus from the slavery of sin and death to the freedom of your justice and peace; may his passover be our passover from this life to life in your presence forever.

April 3: Holy Saturday and Easter Vigil

Lumen Christi

Readings: Gen 1:1–2:2 or 1:1, 26-31a; Gen 22:1-18 or 22:1-2, 9a, 10-13, 15-18; Exod 14:15–15:1; Isa 54:5-14; Isa 55:1-11; Bar 3:9-15, 32–4:4; Ezek 36:16-17a, 18-28; Rom 6:3-11; Luke 24:1-12

Scripture:
[The women] found the stone rolled away from the tomb;
  but when they entered,
  they did not find the body of the Lord Jesus. . . .
  "Why do you seek the living one among the dead?
He is not here, but he has been raised." (Luke 24:3, 5)

Reflection: Tonight's Easter Vigil of the resurrection begins with the blessing and lighting of the large paschal candle. As the vigil begins, its light will transform the church from pitch dark to golden light. The heat of the flame confirms our hope that the transformation of Lenten winter into Easter springtime has been realized; its light reminds us that Christ is the first light of a new creation, a second genesis.

Inserted in the candle are five wax nails that signify the wounds that the crucified Jesus received in his hands, feet, and side. These five wax nails are symbols of the great love of God for us, love so great that he humbled himself and died for us so that he might rise and call us to himself. These marks in the candle remind us that God is with us in our hurts and grief, that God's Spirit of compassion is in our midst in our love and concern for one another transforms such hurt into healing.

The paschal candle will remain lighted throughout the Easter season. It will then be given a place of honor near the baptismal font. During the year, it will be lighted at the celebrations of baptism and at funerals: by its light, we welcome those who are reborn in the waters of baptism; by its light, we commend to God the souls of those who will go before us in peace to the eternal dwelling place of the Father.

The paschal candle reminds us that in every moment of our lives, in every storm that batters our little boat, in every cross we struggle to bear, the Risen Christ is with us, illuminating the way, bearing our crosses with us, assuring us that we are always loved, forgiven, and welcomed by the God who gave us this Easter miracle. Jesus' resurrection is a new day for humanity, a day in which death becomes for us not an end in itself but a passover into the life of God. All that Christ taught is vindicated and affirmed in the Father's raising him from the dead to dwell in our midst always.

Meditation: Remember in the quiet of today those in your life who have been reborn in the waters of baptism and who have gone before us to the dwelling place of God.

Prayer: Risen Christ, may we reflect your light in our love for one another: in washing one another's feet, in helping one another bear our crosses of sorrow and pain, in giving to one another without counting the cost or without expecting anything in return. May your light dispel the darkness of despair and illuminate our lives with Easter hope.

April 4: Easter Sunday

"Let Him Easter in Us"

Readings: Acts 10:34a, 37-43; Col 3:1-4 or 1 Cor 5:6b-8; John 20:1-9 or Luke 24:1-12 or Luke 24:13-35

Scripture:
On the first day of the week,
  Mary of Magdala came to the tomb early in the morning,
  while it was still dark,
  and saw the stone removed from the tomb. . . .
When Simon Peter arrived after [the other disciple],
  he went into the tomb and saw the burial cloths there,
  and the cloth that had covered his head,
  not with the burial cloths but rolled up in a separate
    place. (John 20:1, 6-7)

Reflection: On December 8, 1875, the German ship the *Deutschland* sank in the North Sea, off the English coast. Among the 157 passengers who perished were five Franciscan sisters traveling to Missouri to take up new teaching missions. The young nuns sacrificed their own lives so that others might be rescued. According to one account, the sisters remained below deck as the ship sank. As the water rose around them, they clasped hands and were heard praying, "O Christ, O Christ, come quickly!"

The Jesuit poet Gerard Manley Hopkins was profoundly moved by their story and wrote a poem about the tragedy,

"The Wreck of the *Deutschland*," which he dedicated to the five Franciscans. He saw in their deaths a parallel to the suffering of Christ. Hopkins concludes the poem with this line: "Let him easter in us, be a dayspring to the dimness of us . . ."

Hopkins uses "easter" as a verb; as a nautical term, to "easter" means to steer a craft eastward, into the light.

Easter as a *verb*—not just the name of this great festival we begin today, not just the mystery of God's redemptive love that the gospel can barely articulate, but Easter as something we *think*, something we *feel*, something we *do*.

"Let him easter in us," that we may live in the light of his compassion, peace, justice, and forgiveness.

"Let him easter in us," that we may be a healer like him, a teacher like him, a footwasher like him.

"Let him easter in us," that we may bear our crosses for one another as he bore his cross for us.

"Let him easter in us," that we may, at the end of our voyage, "easter" in him.

Meditation: How can you "do" Easter in the busy-ness of your everyday life?

Prayer: "Easter" in us, O Risen Christ, that your resurrection may become a way of living, a way of loving, a way of seeing and hearing and understanding. Let us "do" Easter every day. May this Easter illuminate our lives with the light of your compassion, justice, and peace.

Acknowledgments

Introduction: From *Aurora Leigh, Book VII* by Elizabeth Barrett Browning.

February 21: Norris, Kathleen. *Dakota: A Spiritual Geography*. New York: Ticknor & Fields, 1993, pp. 17, 18.

February 22: Kushner, Harold S. *Overcoming Life's Disappointments*. New York: Alfred A. Knopf, 2006, p. 35.

March 7: Sheen, Martin. "Martin Sheen: Breaking Through." Interview by Nancy Perry Graham. *AARP Magazine* (July–August 2008).

March 10: McCarthy, Cormac. *The Road*. New York: Vintage International, 2006, pp. 278, 279.

March 12: Frankl, Viktor E. *Man's Search for Meaning*. Rev. ed. New York: Washington Square Press, 1959, 1962, 1984, pp. 137–38.

March 15: Comer, Kim, ed. *Wisdom of the Sadhu: Teachings of Sundar Singh*. Farmington, PA: Plough Publishing House, 2007, pp. 152–53.

March 17: Roy, Denise. *My Monastery Is a Minivan: Where the Daily Is Divine and the Routine Becomes Prayer*. Chicago, IL: Loyola Press, 2001, pp. 88, 3, xvii.

March 22: Taylor, Barbara Brown. *An Altar in the World: A Geography of Faith*. New York: Harper One, 2009, pp. 144, 145.